A Ladybird Book

CONTENTS

Teaching
Reading

by W. MURRAY

Ladybird Books Ltd Loughborough

The teaching of reading and writing

Reading and writing are the basic means to knowledge and culture, and are essential to a full life in a civilised community, but intellectual, moral and emotional growth is of even greater consequence. All teaching should therefore be in the context of child study. A pleasant and understanding teacher-child relationship is the first essential in learning.

Three of the greatest achievements of the human mind are brought together when a child is learning to read and write. Ideas come first as the mind develops, then speech through which ideas flow, and later the ability to record and interpret thinking, through writing and print.

In this pattern of natural development, thought is stimulated if an enriching environment is created within a framework of security. Activities, feelings and interests promote enquiry and encourage the use of language.

The part that language plays in the formation of concepts is of major importance. It is now believed that the genetic potential of intelligence cannot be fully exploited without the use of language.

In the teaching of reading, the emphasis in the past has been on drills and exercises, but reading is now treated as one aspect of a language/arts programme and meaningful reading emphasised. Reading and writing should flow through the natural interests and activities of children. But nothing displaces the book designed to stimulate and interest, and to give adequate practice at the appropriate level, for we learn to read by reading, and to write by writing.

This illustration is from page 15 of book 1a 'Play with us' in the Ladybird Key Words Reading Scheme.

Reading readiness – old ideas and new

We are witnessing great and rapid changes in education, not only in its organisation but also in the curriculum. Methods of learning at all ages are constantly being re-examined.

For about thirty years it has been accepted that, in general, a mental age* of 6 to $6\frac{1}{2}$ years was needed before children could undertake the complex mental activities required in learning to read. It has been recognised that some children learn to read earlier than this, and authorities such as P. Witty, A. I. Gates, D. H. Russell and A. F. Watts qualify their findings on reading readiness. For example, F. J. Schonell wrote in 'The Psychology and Teaching of Reading' . . . 'The consensus of results from educational research indicates that for normal pupils the more formal approach to reading should not begin before a mental age of about six is reached, but, of course, there will be many exceptions to this guide, particularly where other conditions are favourable.'

*'Mental age' queried.

The mental age is worked out from the intelligence quotient, using the formula

$$Mental\ Age = \frac{IQ \times Chronological\ Age}{100}$$

In recent years there has been a considerable change of thought about intelligence, and a greater realisation of the limitations of intelligence testing. Some psychologists and teachers do not now believe that there is such a concept as the 'mental age' of a child, and that its use is a misleading simplification.

Nevertheless, reading readiness and the mental age of $6\frac{1}{2}$ years became linked as a generalisation in the minds of so many that in a 1963 issue of 'Educational Research' the National Foundation for Educational Research called for a re-examination of the reading readiness concept.

In an article entitled 'The Idea of Reading Readiness: a Re-examination', A. E. Sanderson drew attention to the 'loose thinking' surrounding this issue. R. Lynn followed, writing on 'Reading Readiness and the Perceptual Abilities of Young Children'. His concluding paragraph read . . . 'Our conclusion is that sufficient evidence exists to dispose of the theory that children cannot perceive detail accurately until a mental age of 6 to 8. The evidence suggests that accurate perception and learning of whole words are readily accomplished at a mental age of $2\frac{1}{2}$ to $3\frac{1}{2}$ years, and probably earlier. Furthermore, many of the studies cited show that children enjoy this learning. With the disposal of the spurious concept of delayed perceptual maturation, it seems doubtful whether the concept of reading readiness has sufficient substance to be worth retaining.'

In a third article in this series "Is a Mental Age of Six Essential for 'Reading Readiness'?", J. A. Downing re-emphasised that "(1) normal children *can* learn to read at a younger mental age than 6 years, and (2) the necessary mental age for reading readiness is not fixed but is *relative* to the conditions under which the learner operates."

Most teachers and parents feel that safeguards are needed if very young children are to be taught to read. At the present time, some are inclined to suspend judgement as to the value of advancing a child's reading life by two or three years.

A Reading Readiness Questionnaire

Despite the considerable evidence of many more children learning to read earlier, teachers of young children nearly always find some who do not seem ready, or able, to learn to read. These children appear to be physically, intellectually, socially or psychologically too immature to develop the complex skills required. In these cases it is wise to study the previous histories, medical records, intelligence levels, and home backgrounds of the children concerned. Perhaps their basic needs as human beings are not being satisfied. We all need security, social approval, independence and self-esteem. Too much stress can slow down learning or even cause a complete blockage.

The reading readiness guide* which follows may help those in doubt as to whether the learner is ready to learn to read. In most cases there should be satisfactory answers to the majority of the nineteen questions listed, before any formal approach to reading is made.

*From 'Key Words to Literacy' by J. McNally and W. Murray, published by The Schoolmaster Publishing Co. Ltd., Derbyshire House, Kettering, Northants.

The following Reading Readiness Guide should be of special interest to parents who want to teach their pre-school children the first steps in learning to read. It is most important that stress is absent during these earliest reading lessons, that the child learns because he wants to, and that he proceeds at his own pace. Attempts to teach reading to a child who is not ready can cause not only failure but an adverse emotional attitude towards learning.

Reading Readiness Guide

1 Can the child see and hear properly?

2 Is he free from speech defect?

3 Is his general health satisfactory?

4 Are there any other comments of significance on the medical record?

5 Does he appear to be seriously retarded in intelligence?

6 Does he ask questions, does he want to know about the objects and happenings in his environment?

7 Does he understand oral instructions and can he carry them out?

8 Does he listen satisfactorily to a story?

9 Can he re-tell a simple story in fairly logical sequence?

10 Can he see similarities and differences in simple drawings?

11 Does he play constructively with apparatus?

12 Does he draw in a representational form?

13 Has he grown out of babyish behaviour such as baby-talk, temper tantrums, excessive shyness and stubbornness?

14 Is there any evidence that he is being subjected to undue stress and strain?

15 Is he generally self-reliant, e.g. not continually asking for help, and able to work on his own for short periods?

16 Is the home background reasonably satisfactory?

17 Does he co-operate reasonably with others?

18 Can he match word with word?

19 Does he show signs of wanting to read?

Pre-reading activities

If the child is not ready to learn to read, a planned programme of pre-reading activities is advised. This is designed to increase the child's experience, foster the growth of language, ease psychological stress, and encourage awareness and concentration. All this implies a varied and stimulating programme.

Research has shown that reading readiness can be affected by training and is not dependent solely upon maturation.

Some suggestions for classroom and playground pre-reading activities

Use of subjects which release energy and give emotional discharge – in particular

Art, Crafts.

Music, Movement.

Imaginative play.

Educational walks and visits.

The development of the four vocabularies of the child (hearing, speaking, reading and writing), through –

(a) hearing and speaking – listening to teacher and taking part with other children telling stories, news, rhymes, jingles, poetry, giving instructions, playing games (sand, water, group), listening to radio and watching television programmes, dressing up and acting plays (Wendy House), telephoning, taking part in desk games (snap, dice, lotto, dominoes, snakes and ladders, spinning arrow, etc.), sorting and matching by colour/shape/size in various materials, doing jigsaws and playing with constructional toys. Helpful outside games with adventure playgrounds, climbing apparatus, scrambling net, stilts, trampoline, skates, bicycles, rocker, see-saw, swings, ropes, balls, hoops, skittles, cars, push-along toys, etc.

(b) leading to reading, through picture books, pictures in comics, flash-cards (road signs, names of children, commands, etc.), labels, notices, experience chart, wall stories, books made by teacher and child, and, of course, the book corner.

(c) leading to writing through – pictures and patterns with finger and brush paints, patterns with fingers in sand, and pencil on paper, drawing a story in pictures, tracing pictures, own name, etc., adding word to picture.

Notes

1. Practical help towards establishing reading readiness is given in the first section of Workbook 1 of the Ladybird Key Words Reading Scheme (Publishers: Ladybird Books Ltd., Loughborough).

2. A useful guide when dealing with very young or handicapped children is Children's developmental progress *by M. D. Sheridan, published by the National Foundation for Educational Research Publishing Company.*

The basic fundamentals in learning to read and write

The child's ability to read and write, and the rate of progress of the learner depend on:

(a) *MATURITY AND INTELLIGENCE*
We should bear in mind here the enormously wide

variability in physical and intellectual maturity amongst children of the same age*.

(b) *LANGUAGE / EXPERIENCE BACKGROUND*

This is provided by a stimulating environment in which two-way verbal communication is encouraged.

(c) *THE OPPORTUNITY TO LEARN*

This implies –

1. Reasonable health.
2. Motivation – the teacher should ensure that the child wants to learn.
3. Daily lessons, when the learner is rested and alert.
4. Material geared to the child's interests and ability.

(d) *ABSENCE OF EMOTIONAL STRAIN*

Strain of any kind wastes energy and distracts attention.

(e) *STRENGTH OF VISUAL AND AUDITORY MEMORIES*

It is well known that these vary with individuals, but it is sometimes not realised that memory can be strengthened considerably with regular practice.

*Note

The first word can be spoken by normal children anywhere between 10 months and three years of age. The onset of puberty has a range of 5 years. It is to be expected that the ages at which children learn to read will also vary widely.

An easy approach to reading

It is to be expected that the first words the child learns will be those intimately concerned with his own environment. He will learn to read his own name, the name of the street or road where he lives, such words as OPEN, CLOSED, DANGER, etc., as these words have important meanings for him and are seen daily. It is unavoidable that some of the letters in such words are capitals, but no difficulties arise at this time as the words are learned by a 'whole' approach and not by letters or sounds. In this earliest stage, the emphasis is on reading, not writing.

Constructing an Experience Chart

Continuing the 'natural' approach in the classroom, the teacher often uses an Experience Chart to re-capture interest, to encourage the use of language, to involve all members of the group, and to link other pleasurable activities (e.g. drawing, colouring, cutting out, matching) with reading and writing. Thus, the 'whole word' method is linked with the 'sentence' method or the 'thought getting process', as it is sometimes called.

The teacher guides the discussion about an interesting experience the class or group has had and writes on the board some words as they arise in conversation. Then, again with the help of the class or group, she constructs simple sentences about the experience, using the words on the board. This is done on large cards or sheets of thick paper and illustrations by teacher and children are added. The chart has a title, and the simple sentences are on separate lines. The writing is in large, rounded script.

The children read the Experience Chart as a whole, some with help and some without. Then they match words, phrases and sentences (on separate cards) with the chart. After a few days, the chart is filed for future use. The word cards can be kept in alphabetical order for use with later charts.

A similar approach may be followed with wall stories, projects and centres of interest.

It is repeated that the names and sounds of letters are not emphasised at this stage. The whole word (in the 'whole word' or 'look-say' methods) or the sentence (in the 'sentence' method) are presented directly to the child, who learns the words by their shape, context and repetition.

Other words in the classroom

The classroom walls and furniture show other words, phrases and sentences which reflect more of the children's interests and activities. The teacher is careful not to have too many word cards on view at the same time.

In a typical classroom for young children, some of the following might be seen – the names of objects, a list of classroom duties, the days of the week, a weather chart, labels for children to wear, the names of the children in the class and the name of the teacher, the name of the school and town, a nursery rhyme.

The Sentence Method

There are about 2,800 languages in the world, and a great number of different ways of learning to read. Although reading is a complex activity, the human brain is so adaptable that it is even possible for a deaf and dumb child to learn to read. There is a case on record of a blind and armless child who learned to read by tracing with his nose.

The most commonly used initial method of teaching reading in this country and the world is the 'sentence' method. Surveys in 46 countries by the International Bureau of Education and the United Nations Educational Scientific and Cultural Organisation show that the 'sentence' method is the most generally recommended, and is often the initial method used even where the language of the country is purely phonetic.

In 'The Teaching of Reading and Writing – An International Survey' (UNESCO and Evans Bros, 1956), William S. Gray writes: "If the 'sentence' method is well applied, it lays the foundation of practically all the attitudes and skills required for good reading – a thoughtful reading attitude, a clear grasp of meaning, accuracy and independence in word recognition, intelligent reaction to what is read, application of the ideas acquired, and interest in learning. When the reader advances beyond the initial stages, he is not faced with the difficulties of adjusting himself to a new set of reading attitudes; instruction develops the attitudes and skills already implanted, improving and extending them. This ensures uninterrupted growth and makes for economy and efficiency."

As F. J. Schonell wrote in his 'Psychology and Teaching of Reading' (Oliver and Boyd, 1960) — "It is reassuring to record the great advances that have been made in recent years in the teaching of reading through increased use of whole word/sentence methods, employing attractive and meaningful reading. That millions of children, and hitherto illiterate adults, have gained skill and joy through the use of reading schemes based on the psychologically sound whole-word/sentence methods is one of the outstanding educational achievements of the century."

Statistics given in '11,000 Seven Year Olds' (The First Report of the National Child Development Study, for the Central Advisory Council for Education) show that nearly 70% of the teachers interviewed do not use the sounds of letters (i.e. the 'phonic' method) in the *initial* stages of learning to read.

Blending in the Phonic Method

Most reading schemes use 'sentence', 'look-say' or 'whole word' methods in their first stages. With these, the child soon becomes confident in his growing ability to learn to read, if the words are introduced gradually, with interest and adequate repetition. Then, when rather more than one hundred words are known by these 'whole' approaches, the 'phonic' method is also used, to give an additional means of getting to know new words.

The 'phonic' method is used in the teaching of reading because with 'regular' words, the sounds of letters (not their names) when uttered rapidly (or 'blended') produce the words. English is not a purely phonetic language, so care must be taken in presenting this method to the learner.

Too much emphasis on the phonic method, especially if used too early in the reading programme, can slow down progress and harm the attitude towards reading. W. S. Gray investigated for UNESCO the most commonly used methods of the teaching of reading, and his book summarised the evidence for and against each. He made criticisms of the 'phonic' method, which have led to the development of a more imaginative and pleasurable approach to this 'synthetic' method, as it is called. Schonell considered that the phonic method "interferes with the idea of grasping words, phrases and sentences as meaningful language units". Dr. Joyce Morris in 'Reading in the Primary School', summarised by writing . . . "Apart from any consideration of language irregularities, most educationists in English-speaking countries today consider that synthetic methods for beginning reading are psychologically unsound. Consequently, they advocate a 'whole-word' approach to reading, followed at a later stage by some phonic instruction according to individual needs. In modern reading programmes, therefore, the importance of 'readiness' and 'reading for meaning' is stressed, and less emphasis than before is placed upon systematic phonic training", and later . . . "Most educationists suggest that systematic phonic instruction should be delayed until children have acquired a good vocabulary and developed an interest in reading as a means of obtaining information and enjoyment . . ."

The Learner-centred approach for the individual child

The 'learner-centred' approach may be used when the teacher can give a considerable time every day to each child. When there is time to study each individual, the teacher can construct a reading and writing programme to reflect the enjoyable aspects of the learner's own life.

In such an initial reading programme, the first reader can be a personal book made by teacher and child. This book can draw together in pictorial form the learner's own interests and pleasurable activities, and introduce him to a few words which arise directly from them. These words are few in number, written in clear, rounded script, and are given as much repetition as possible in the book, while holding the interest. They are taught by 'whole' methods, i.e. by 'look-say', 'whole word' or 'sentence' methods.

The child is encouraged to read his book not only to his teacher, but to his friends and family. Thus, in a happy atmosphere in which praise and encouragement are given freely, a healthy attitude towards learning is formed.

This approach may be continued to embody topic and interest books of various shapes and sizes, all self-made by individuals and groups, under the guidance of the teacher. For example, 'My House' is a popular book to make, especially if the card cover is cut in the shape of a house and door and windows drawn on it. Each page might represent a different room, with coloured drawings of furniture and people, and words underneath. 'My Family', 'Our Pet(s)', 'Rhymes I Like', 'Things We Grow', 'My Holiday', 'My Friends', 'Things I Like' are the kinds of interesting and popular topics which may be developed in this way.

Three books at once

There is common agreement that there should be at least three books in the life of the child who is learning to read.

The first is the one the teacher reads to the class or group.* Besides giving the child pleasure and interest and encouraging him to listen carefully, story reading helps to develop a love of books and a desirable attitude towards reading. This book, carefully chosen by the teacher, gives the child his first glimpse of the wonderful world of literature awaiting him once he has achieved reading skill. Discussion often follows a reading lesson of this kind, and during this the teacher guides the child towards critical thinking.

The second book is the one in the chosen reading scheme. It is important that this is matched to the level of ability of the child, and that he should enjoy using it. Linked with this there can be the workbook, reading games and apparatus of various kinds, employing in the main the vocabulary of the reading book.

The third book is the free choice one from the attractively set-out book corner. Here a wide variety of colourful and interesting books are displayed so that the front cover of each is seen. Some of the appeal is lost if books are closely stacked so that only the spines are shown. Plenty of space should be allocated to this book exhibition, and some kind of grading is necessary. One section should show picture books without words, or with very few words, to cater for the beginner.

*The Ladybird 'Well-loved Tales' are useful here. These are well-known stories, re-told by V. Southgate, M.A., B.Com.

What is a reading scheme?

A reading scheme is a specially designed series of books to teach reading. The books are written on a controlled vocabulary so that the new words are introduced gradually, have a high rate of repetition and are carried over to following books in the series. The best schemes are written with the aid of control charts, to ensure a scientific word control. In such schemes the new words introduced on each page are indicated, and the rate of repetition is given in the notes for teachers. Occasionally a reading scheme is based on the accepted findings of research.

The first books are generally written on very few words, and are well illustrated to aid understanding and to make the books attractive. The rate of introduction of new words increases throughout the scheme, and the total number of words used is generally between one and two thousand. Writing forms an important part of most schemes, and is almost always linked with comprehensive exercises.

Many children are able to learn to read from books, without the use of supporting apparatus. However, apparatus is useful with some children, particularly when in large classes.

The following are the most popular items of supporting apparatus for the early stages of a reading scheme:

1 Workbooks.
2 Wall pictures, with linking phrase or sentence cards.
3 Outline picture pads.
4 Colouring and tracing books.
5 Flash cards, large and small.
6 Picture-word matching cards.

7 Picture-sentence matching cards.

8 Picture Dictionaries

The teaching of reading with a reading scheme is described in the following pages. An outline of the chosen reading scheme is given first.

THE LADYBIRD KEY WORDS READING SCHEME

The scientific basis

The author and publishers of this reading scheme rate highly the artistic appeal of a book. Therefore, much attention has been given to the layout and the plentiful provision of colourful illustrations. Emphasis has also been put on a scientific approach, developed to ensure rapid learning.

The scientific basis of the reading scheme is the use of 'Key Words'*. This is the name given to a group of the most used words of the language. Research has established that a relatively few English words form a very high proportion of those in every-day use. The diagrams printed on the following pages indicate this, and show how these words have been applied to the Ladybird Key Words Reading Scheme to accelerate progress.

The early books of the scheme are written with the 300 Key Words (i.e. the 250 of the basic list plus the 50 'reserve' words) and the rest of the books bring the learner's reading vocabulary up to 1,934 words.

Children learn to read more quickly and easily if the first words are those in common daily use, presented in an attractive learning situation, with a carefully planned programme.

*See 'Key Words to Literacy'.

Two diagrams showing the number of words in the vocabulary of an average adult, and the importance of Key Words.

This square, and the one below, each represents 20,000 words which is an estimate of the number of words in the vocabulary of an average adult.

The total of these three sections shows that 100 words make up ½ of those in common use

the first 12 Key Words make up ¼ of those we read and write

the next 20

68 more words

a further 150

¾ line would mark limit of 300 key words if applied to juvenile reading

19,750 words

24

The application of Key Words to the Ladybird Key Words Reading Scheme.

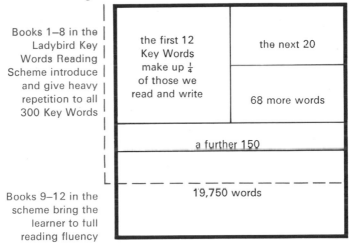

Books 1–8 in the Ladybird Key Words Reading Scheme introduce and give heavy repetition to all 300 Key Words

the first 12 Key Words make up $\frac{1}{4}$ of those we read and write

the next 20

68 more words

a further 150

19,750 words

Books 9–12 in the scheme bring the learner to full reading fluency

In this scheme the rate of introduction of new words has been kept low and the number of repetitions high, especially in the early stages. There is a complete carry-over of new words to the following book, up to stage eight in the scheme.

There are three parallel sets of books (a, b and c), each set consisting of twelve carefully graded books with full colour illustrations throughout. All three sets are written with the same controlled vocabulary up to and including stage nine, with additional phonic words added to the 'c' set from Book 4c onwards.

The early books are in large print and the simplified forms of a, g and I are used. Words new to the text on each page are also printed at the foot of the page for easy reference. A list of all the words new to each book is given at the back of every copy, where there is also to be found a summary of the control chart.

How the scheme works

In Book 1a, the learner meets only sixteen different words, with an average of ten repetitions per word. He then reads Book 1b to find the same sixteen words, but in different context and with different illustrations. Moving on to Book 1c, he again finds the same sixteen words (with four instructional words added), but this time in a writing context. Writing helps reading greatly.

Having completed the first stage (Books 1a, 1b and 1c), the learner progresses to Books 2a, 2b, 2c, and so on throughout the scheme. Phonic teaching is included from Books 4c to 11c.

The suggested areas of use for the supplementary teaching material supplied is as follows:

Wall pictures and sentence cards	⎫
Picture-Word Matching cards	⎪
Picture-Sentence Matching cards	⎬ Books 1 to 3
Outline picture pads	⎪
Colouring and Tracing book	⎭
Workbooks	Books 1 to 6
Flash cards, large and small	Books 1 to 6
Key Words Card	Books 3 to 8
Individual Record Card	Throughout the scheme
The Reading Test card forms part of the Individual Record Card, and covers	Books 1 to 6
Picture Dictionaries	Books 1 to 8

Using the reading scheme

Some teachers use the wall pictures, sentence cards and flash cards of a reading scheme before they introduce the first reader to the class or group. Others use these large pictures and cards at the same time as the children are beginning the first book. A third group of teachers dispenses with the use of wall pictures and cards, starting their teaching of reading with the first book. If a reading scheme is flexible, it can be made to suit any of these three approaches.

In deciding her own method, the teacher is influenced by her training and the environment in which she finds herself. She may be faced with a large class of very young children from relatively poor homes. Alternatively, her school may be in a well-to-do area, with bright children, and by good fortune her reception class may be comparatively small.

For demonstration purposes let us imagine that the teacher has a large group of children, most of whom have not been introduced to the printed word. She puts an attractive and interesting wall picture in front of the children and encourages them to talk about it. The coloured picture shows a happy boy and girl who are using a swing on a sunny day. After a while she introduces the names of the two children in the picture, and then produces a long card on which are printed the three words

| Peter and Jane |

She points to each word as she reads it, moving her hand from left to right across the card. The children are learning the three words and are also having training in the left to right eye movement necessary in reading. This is not a *natural* eye habit.

Three separate cards are then produced, each bearing one of the words `Peter` `and` `Jane` These are arranged in the same order as those on the long card. Verbalisation continues throughout. A second long card is then put up. This reads `Jane and Peter` Again the teacher points and reads, and again the three separate word cards are arranged, this time to match the second long card. Pages 6 to 11 in Book 1a ('Play with us') may then be shown and read. These contain only the three words dealt with in this first simple lesson. For a longer lesson, the content of pages 12 to 15 could be included. These pages teach two more words — **here, is.** Two sentence cards `Peter is here` and `Jane is here` are available, and several of the wall pictures suit the words. The separate `is` and `here` are also needed.

There are six sets of wall pictures in the Ladybird Key Words Reading Scheme. Each set contains six pictures with two linking phrase or sentence cards per picture. Sets 1 and 2 are for use with Book 1a, sets 3 and 4 with Book 2a, and sets 5 and 6 with Book 3a.

The large flash cards provided are in two sets and cover all the vocabulary in the first six books of the reading scheme. 120 double-sided cards are in each set. Similar sets of small flash cards are also available.

Tapes linked with the first six books of the Scheme have been prepared, tapes 1a and 2a having been specially designed to encourage modulation and expressive phrasing.

A boxed set of 16 different reading games is also available.

The use of wall pictures and flash cards is optional

Which are the Key Words?

Here are the 'Key Words', the most used words in English, applied to the vocabulary of the average person:

12

**a and he
I in is
it of that
the to was**

all as at be but are for had have him his not on one said so they we with you₂₀

about an back been before big by call came can come could did do down first from get go has her here if into just like little look made make me more much must my no new now off only or our over other out right see she some their them then there this two up want well went who were what when where which will your old ₆₈

After Again Always Am Ask Another Any Away Bad Because Best Bird Black Blue Boy Bring Day Dog Don't Eat Every Fast Father Fell Find Five Fly Four Found Gave Girl Give Going Good Got Green Hand Head Help Home House How Jump Keep Know Last Left Let Live Long Man Many May Men Mother Mr. Never Next Once Open Own Play Put Ran Read Red Room Round Run Sat Saw Say School Should Sing Sit Soon Stop Take Tell Than These Thing Think Three Time Too Tree Under Us Very Walk White Why Wish Work Woman Would Yes Year Bus Apple Baby Bag Ball Bed Book Box Car Cat Children Cow Cup Dinner Doll Door Egg End Farm Fish Fun Hat Hill Horse Jam Letter Milk Money Morning Mrs. Name Night Nothing Picture Pig Place Rabbit Road Sea Shop Sister Street Sun Table Tea Today Top Toy Train Water ₁₅₀

This area represents 19.750 further words. Space does not permit the printing of these words.

The diagram represents the 20,000 words in an average vocabulary. The frequency of use of the Key Words is indicated by area, and also to some extent by the size of the print used.

The reading books

The use of apparatus with a reading scheme is optional. Apparatus is helpful, especially with large classes, but its use is not essential.

The main core of the reading programme is the series of graded books written on a controlled vocabulary. As has been explained, in the Ladybird Key Words Reading Scheme there are 36 readers, presented in three graded sets. These are set out below.

Number of different words new to the book	Book	Book	Book	Reading Age
16	1a ———→	1b ————	→1c(+4)	4 - $4\frac{1}{2}$
27	2a	2b	2c(+3)	$4\frac{1}{2}$ - 5
30	3a	3b	3c	5 - $5\frac{1}{2}$
41	↓4a	4b	4c*	$5\frac{1}{2}$ - 6
46	5a	5b	5c*	6 - $6\frac{1}{2}$
52	6a	6b	6c*	$6\frac{1}{2}$ - 7
67	7a	7b(+1)	7c*	7 - $7\frac{1}{2}$
91	8a	8b	8c*	$7\frac{1}{2}$ - 8
110	9a	9b	9c*	8 - $8\frac{1}{2}$
115	10a	10b(+54)	10c*	$8\frac{1}{2}$ - 9
129	11a	11b(+77)	11c*	9 - $9\frac{1}{2}$
126	12a	12b(+132)	12c*	$9\frac{1}{2}$ - 10

Plus additional phonic words (total 815)

Overall total of different words in the scheme 1,934

The above table lists the approximate reading ages of the books. Reading fluency will have been achieved when the learner has worked through all the 36 books. The figures in the left-hand column indicate the vocabulary loading at each stage.

As each set up to stage 9 is written on the same vocabulary (with phonic words added in the 'c' series from 4c onwards), the teacher can start one group reading an 'a' book, while another group has the parallel 'b' book. The books can then be interchanged between groups. This economises on the number of books needed – an important point for teachers whose funds are limited.

The Workbooks 1 to 6 use the same vocabulary as the Readers 1 to 6.

The link between reading and writing

Writing is taught for its own sake, of course. Writing also helps greatly when the child is learning to read, if the same vocabulary is used. Books 1 to 10 in the 'c' series of this reading scheme teach the learner to write, using the parallel vocabulary of the 'a' and 'b' books. There are 130 pages of writing exercises linked with pictures. Answers are given in the backs of the books to encourage self-marking.

In the very first stage, every possible assistance is given to the learner. The maximum amount of pictorial aid is provided, and the large print in the books is similar to the rounded script the teacher uses. The word to be written by the child is close by a copy of the same word, except on a few later pages where known words are used. The first three books conclude with several pages of simple jumbled sentences with pictorial clues. Some teachers allow slower children to use small flash cards with these exercises, arranging the word cards in correct order before writing.

From Book 4c onwards, the writing exercises assist

the learning of the phonic sounds being taught.

Further help with reading and writing is given in Workbooks 1 to 6, which are an optional part of the first six stages of the reading scheme.

Note

Very young or handicapped children cannot learn to write as quickly as they learn to read. In these cases the learners should work through the 'c' series at their own pace, while proceeding more quickly with the parallel readers in the 'a' and 'b' series.

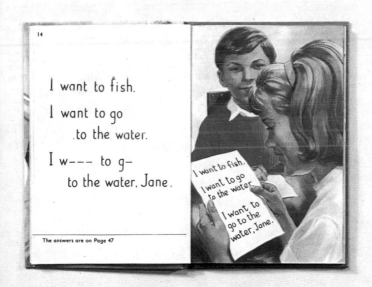

Workbooks

The workbooks in a reading scheme are designed to give the learner a number of pleasurable experiences with reading and writing. In each workbook there are tracing, drawing and colouring exercises linked with words, phrases and sentences from the parallel reader or readers. Matching exercises, games and puzzles are sometimes included. The learner works *in* the workbook provided, so in this sense it is consumable.

The teacher may give the child a particular workbook to use before the parallel reader is begun, while it is in use or after it has been read. However, in general, workbooks are used as the learner is progressing through the accompanying reader.

There are six workbooks in the Ladybird Key Words Reading Scheme, one for each of the first six stages. Thus Workbook 1 is used with Books 1a, 1b and 1c, Workbook 2 with Books 2a, 2b, 2c and so on.

Workbook 1 is unusual in that the first section contains a reading readiness guide. The reading readiness questionnaire given on pages 9 and 10 of this book is reproduced for the teacher, and six pages of illustrations are provided for use with it. The rest of this workbook is concerned with the vocabulary of the Books 1a, 1b and 1c, and a reading test based on this is given at the end.

Instructions for the use of the workbooks are given on the inside covers, and a letter formation guide appears in Workbooks 2 to 6.

Workbooks are popular with children, and their use helps towards forming a desirable attitude of pleasure and confidence towards learning to read and write.

Applying the Phonic Method

The teaching of phonics in the Ladybird Key Words Reading Scheme is given in Books 4c to 11c. The approach used ensures that:

1 Phonic teaching is introduced after an enjoyable and successful start to reading has been made by sentence and whole word methods.

2 Phonic instruction is given initially on words already known to the learner.

3 Maximum pictorial aid is provided.

4 A variety of interesting approaches is employed which gives disguised repetition.

5 Writing is used to assist retention of the sounds taught.

6 The sounds are applied to a meaningful reading situation directly they are learned.

The sounds are presented in the following order:

Book 4c and Workbook 4 .. b, c, t, a, f, h, m, s

Book 5c and Workbook 5 .. i, e, o, u, d, g, l, n

Book 6c and Workbook 6 .. p, r, w, j, k, v, x, y, z, qu

Book 7c .. ee, oo, ing, sh, ea, ch, er, ll, -e, th, wh.

Book 8c .. ai, ay, oa, st, nd, ow, aw, -ce, ck, ar.

Book 9c .. -y, ed, tr, cr, -le, -mp, oy, oi, ir, ur, -nk, br, or.

Book 10c .. -ew, bl, -bb, ou, -ss, gr, -igh, -dd, -rr, -ie, silent k.

Book 11c .. Three sounds of ed, two sounds of ow, three sounds of o, soft c, soft g, variations of ar, er, or, our.

The phonic books in the Ladybird Key Words Reading Scheme 37

Examples are given below and in the following pages of some of the methods used to present the phonic sounds taught in Book 4c 'Say the sound'. This book introduces the phonic approach in the Ladybird Key Words Reading Scheme.

(a) The four words — boy, ball, boat and bus, are already known to the learner from earlier books. After reading them again on page 4 of Book 4c, he is encouraged to look at the pictures opposite and make the initial sound of the words they represent. Tracing round the large printed letter with his finger as he makes the sound helps to fix the memory. This approach is continued on the next two pages with the sound of 'c'.

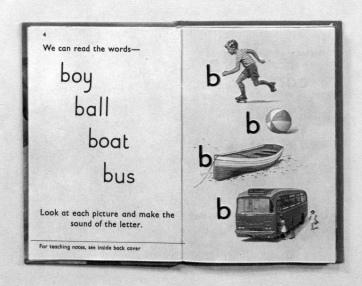

(b) The child writes in his exercise book the eight words listed, choosing which initial sound is needed to complete each word. In this he is helped by the pictorial clue given opposite. On completion of the exercise he turns to page 50 in Book 4c and marks his own work from the answers given there.

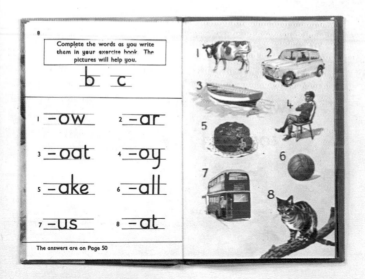

(c) The children are encouraged to cut out small pictures of objects from old picture books, magazines, etc., and to paste them in a scrapbook. Each picture is stuck on a page which bears a letter giving the initial sound of the item pictured.

Four of the sounds taught in Book 4c are applied here in a meaningful learning situation. After reading the text on page 44, the children write out and complete the four sentences printed below it. They then mark their own work from the answers given on page 51.

The children all help to make a big fire at the farm. The man lets the boys and girls have some things for the fire.

"We do not want to get into danger," says Jane to the little girl. "We will keep away."

"There will be no danger," says Peter.

Copy out and complete—

1. The children are —t the farm.

2. They —ake a big fire.

3. The man —elps the children.

4. He gives the children —ome things for the fire.

The answers are on Page 51

'Phonic Pockets' is the name sometimes given to the piece of apparatus seen in use on pages 5 and 7 of Book 5c, 'More sounds to say'. Each child tries to put a picture card into the correct pocket so that the sound of the letter shown is the same as the initial sound of the object pictured. In this instance the two children are working a revision exercise on the sounds learned in Book 4c.

Reproduced below are pages 4 and 5 from Book 7c 'Easy to sound', the fourth of eight phonic books in the Ladybird Key Words Reading Scheme.

It is shown that the sound of 'ee' is taught from a known word 'see' (the sounds s-ee make see).

Then the learner is led to make a word new to him from two known sounds, i.e. b-ee bee.

He then reads four sentences about the bee, helped by the pictures. Further pages give more repetition of the sound of 'ee'.

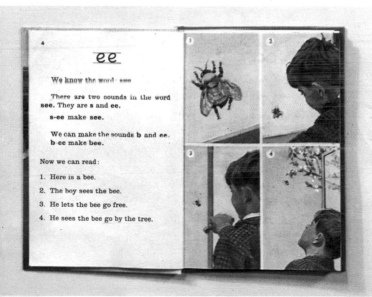

1 A First Ladybird Key Words Picture Dictionary

Ninety-two Key Words are presented in this book, set out in alphabetical order. The words are in extra large print on the left-hand pages, each by a black and white illustration. On the opposite pages are larger illustrations in full colour with the word printed clearly by each picture.

2 A Second Ladybird Key Words Picture Dictionary

All three hundred Key Words are listed in alphabetical order in this Second Picture Dictionary. Each word appears also in a sentence which is illustrated in colour to explain the meaning. All sentences are made up entirely of Key Words, and can be used as an aid in teaching or testing reading, writing or spelling.

3 The Key Words Card

All the Key Words have been printed in alphabetical order on a folded card, which opens out to $9\frac{1}{2}'' \times 13\frac{1}{2}''$ for use on the desk. On the reverse side of the card there are 64 small illustrations, each with the word printed underneath.

The card may be used for a spelling guide when the learner is writing. There are spaces provided for other words to be written in by child or teacher.

The order of the letters of the alphabet may be learned from the card, at the appropriate stage. As all 300 words are presented at the opening of the card, it would not be brought into use while the learner was in the earliest stages of learning to read and write.

1

boat	
boats	
book	
books	
box	
boy	
boys	

2

a
about
after
afternoon
again
all
always
am
an
and
another
any
apple

1. The boy is reading a book **about** cars.

2. The boy runs **after** the bull.

3. It is **afternoon** and the boy is reading **again**.

4. **All** the apples in the box are green.

5. Apples are not **always** green. I **am** eating an **apple and** it is red. I have **another** one in my left hand. Can you see **any** other red apples?

3

KEY WORDS to reading, writing and spelling

The Ladybird Key Words Reading Scheme

KEY WORDS CARD

Some reading difficulties

The Ladybird Key Words Reading Scheme has been carefully constructed to give maximum help to the learner, especially during the initial stages, and if the scheme is properly applied, it will be successful with any child who, in the normal sense, is ready to read. Many millions of the books have been bought since the scheme was first issued, and the great many letters received by the publishers and the author have shown that an unusually high percentage of young children have learned to read with them. Successful learning with the books is also frequently reported by teachers of children previously thought to be backward, and even from Training Centres where so-called 'ineducable' children are now being taught to read.

Nevertheless, some reading difficulties may be found amongst handicapped children, with others whose education has been broken by frequent absences or changes of school, with children who have had severe psychological disturbance, or where some other unusual factor is present. The notes which follow offer help for those cases.

The need for teacher/parent co-operation

With a severe case of reading disability, the teacher is first advised to re-study the reading readiness questionnaire and the list of pre-reading activities. A study of all available medical evidence should be made and consultation between teacher and parent should follow.

Language and intelligence

In the Plowden Report it is stated — "The development of language is central to the educational process. Poverty of language is a major cause of poor achievement". P. E. Vernon states that . . . "Intelligence could hardly develop without this tool (language) that the growing child acquires from the society in which he is reared." He also makes the comment – "Intelligence operates in a context of personality and especially in a framework of motivation and learned behaviour."

Thus happiness and the flow of language are the first aim with the child who has been having difficulty.

Laziness

Insight into laziness may sometimes be gained by considering a list of personality reactions to failure. Amongst these symptoms there commonly appears not only aggression, hypertension and compensation, but withdrawal and defeat. These last two may be mistaken for laziness.

C. Burt's views on laziness are interesting. He suggests it can be caused by physical ill health, intellectual mal-adjustment, an apathetic temperament, an unstable temperament or some form of neurotic disturbance. Thus the underlying cause must be discovered and dealt with. Meanwhile it is advisable to introduce the 'play-way' into the 'backward' classroom . . . and later to build up gradually habits of hard work and dogged perseverance in the face of difficulty and failure. P. A. Witty and D. Kopel state in 'Reading and the Educative Process' . . . "Fully 50% of seriously retarded readers are characterised by fears and anxieties so serious and far-reaching that no programme of re-education could possibly succeed which did not aim to re-establish self-confidence and to remove anxieties."

The non-starter

Because of an adverse emotional overlay, the child

may be against the learning situation and apparently unable to read even a very few simple words. Help may be given here by an attractive reading game using a few pictures with corresponding words. These are given heavy repetition in a pleasurable atmosphere in which incentive is supplied. A good example of this type of reading aid is the 'Football' game, as pictured on page 23 of the publication 'Key Words to Literacy'. For beginners it is best played with six word cards, each with the appropriate illustration on the reverse of the card. When a word is read correctly (checked with the picture), the 'football' is moved one space towards the 'goal'. Two opposing players take turns to read the presented word. The same words learned here can appear in other reading games and also in the individual book made with the learner. The next stage would be Workbook 1, followed by Readers 1a, 1b and 1c.

Reading words backwards

All children have this fault in varying degree during the early stages of learning to read, and it is easily corrected.

To read English the eye must learn the unnatural habit of moving systematically from left to right across the page. This is done in several movements per line, and the words read while the eye is still. Regressions (i.e. moving the eye from right to left) are made by all learners as they puzzle out pronunciation and meaning. These regressions sometimes lead to reading a word backwards, so that 'on' is read as 'no', 'saw' for 'was' or even 'leg' for 'angel'. The more difficult the reading matter for the beginner, the more regressions he will make and the greater the likelihood of reversals.

Give the child easier reading material so that the number of regressions are lessened as the eye moves more easily from left to right. In acute cases allow pointing with the finger, or even drawing a paper across the word or line from left to right.

Reading a new word

After the initial stages of learning, it is advisable for the child to develop as soon as possible the ability to read new words for himself. In training him to do this, it is as well to remember the most common ways of 'unlocking' new words. These are generally thought to be:

1. Using a pictorial clue.
2. Recognising the shape or pattern of the word.
3. Using the context clue – knowledge of the other words in the sentence gives the meaning of the new word.
4. Remembering special features of the word – for example, some words containing 'oo' are easily re-called. Or perhaps the word 'window', as it begins and ends with the same distinctive letter.
5. Noticing a similarity to a word already known – if the child knows 'fish', he may find it easy to learn the word 'wish'. 'Make' helps him to learn 'cake'.
6. Knowing smaller words within the larger new word. If he knows 'after', he may learn 'afternoon' more easily.
7. Using phonetic analysis – the applying of known sounds to the new word.

Remembering the sounds

Some children find real difficulty in remembering the sounds of letters or groups of letters, and it may be wise to delay phonic instruction with them for a longer period than usual.

Others can be led into phonic learning more easily by the popular game 'I spy . . . ' in which the guesser is given the sound of the first letter of the word which represents the chosen object in view. The 'Phonic Teacher' and the 'Phonic Word Jigsaws' (card apparatus supplied by James Galt & Co. Ltd., of Cheadle, Cheshire) are useful and popular, giving repetition in an enjoyable context.

Incentives to write

The 'c' books of the Ladybird Key Words Reading Scheme start very simply by giving one word writing exercises linked with easy comprehension and a pictorial clue. In the first stages the learner is supplied with a copy of the word to be written, in the same shaped letters he is using. The parallel workbooks have dotted outlines of the same words to guide his hand.

As the child progresses, he could also be supplied with a 'free' exercise book in which to write, draw, or trace whatever he likes. With a retarded child, this often helps to overcome inhibitions caused through previous failures.

Later, the usual letter and note-writing to his friends can be expanded by writing to the Queen, television and sports personalities and the like, pen friends and/or an adopted ship. The Commonwealth Institute (Kensington High Street, London W8 6NQ) can supply information about the Commonwealth, catalogues of books and craft-work on sale. Replies and samples can be obtained from The British Trades Alphabet (Wakefield Road, Leeds 10). 'The Treasure Chest for Teachers' (Schoolmaster Publishing Co. Ltd.) supplies a valuable descriptive list of services available to teachers and schools.

Purposeful writing generally awakens interest and often stimulates enthusiasm.

Individual Record and Reading Test Card

The Ladybird Key Words Reading Scheme Individual Record Card and Reading Test provides an easy-to-keep record of books read, with space for notes by the teacher. The Reading Test, which is on the reverse side of the Card and covers the first six stages of the Scheme, has identical letter shapes and print sizes to those found in the books.

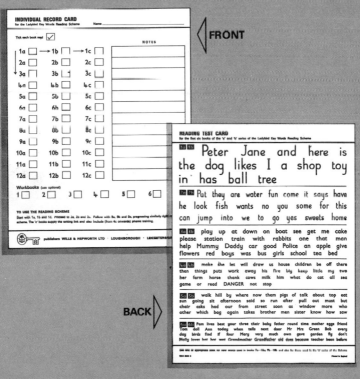

Bibliography

"Reading in Modern Education."
    P. Witty. D. C. Heath & Co.

"The Improvement of Reading."
    A. I. Gates. Macmillan.

"Children Learn to Read."
    D. H. Russell. Ginn.

"The Language and Mental Development of Children."
    A. F. Watts. Harrap.

"The Psychology and Teaching of Reading."
    F. J. Schonell. Oliver & Boyd.

"Educational Research."
    Published termly for the National Foundation for Educational Research.

"Key Words to Literacy."
    J. McNally and W. Murray. Schoolmaster Pub. Co.

"Children's developmental progress."
    M. D. Sheridan. National Foundation for Educational Research Pub. Co.

"The Teaching of Reading."
    Publication 113 of U.N.E.S.C.O. and the International Bureau of Education.

"The Teaching of Reading and Writing – an international survey."
    U.N.E.S.C.O. and Evans Bros.

"11,000 Seven Year Olds."
    Longmans for the Central Advisory Council for Education.

"Reading in the Primary School."
    J. M. Morris. Newnes for N.F.E.R.

"Children and their Primary Schools." Volumes 1 and 2.
    A report to the Central Advisory Council for Education. H.M.S.O.

"Intelligence and Attainment tests."
    P. E. Vernon. University of London Press.

"The Backward Child."
    C. Burt. University of London Press.

"Reading and the Educative Process."
    P. Witty and D. Kopel. Ginn.

"Early Stages." Catalogue.
    James Galt & Co.